STEM Miles[...]
Historic Inventions a[...]

CHARLES DARWIN AND THE ORIGIN OF SPECIES

Eileen S. Coates

PowerKiDS
press.

New York

Published in 2019 by The Rosen Publishing Group, Inc.
29 East 21st Street, New York, NY 10010

Editor: Tanya Dellaccio
Book Design: Reann Nye

Photo Credits: Cover, p. 1 Dorling Kindersley/Getty Images; p. 5 Bob Thomas/ Popperfoto/Getty Images; p. 6 https://commons.wikimedia.org/wiki/File: Charles_Darwin_1816.jpg; p. 7 Mondadori Portfolio/Hulton Fine Art Collection/ Getty Images; p. 9 (top) https://en.wikipedia.org/wiki/File:Christ%27s_College_ First_Court,_Cambridge,_UK_-_Diliff.jpg; p. 9 (bottom) Loop Images/Universal Images Group/Getty Images; pp. 11, 19 UniversalImagesGroup/Universal Images Group/Getty Images; p. 12 Boyd Hendrikse/Shutterstock.com; p. 13 Ryan M. Bolton/Shutterstock.com; p. 14 Ralph Lee Hopkins/NationalGeographic/Getty Images; p. 15 Print Collector/Hulton Fine Art Collection/Getty Images; p. 17 (top) https://commons.wikimedia.org/wiki/File:Charles_Darwin_seated.jpg; p. 17 (bottom) John Phillips/UK Press/Getty Images; p. 18 Print Collector/Hulton Archive/ Getty Images; p. 21 Bettmann/Getty Images.

Library of Congress Cataloging-in-Publication Data

Names: Coates, Eileen S., author.
Title: Charles Darwin and the origin of species / Eileen S. Coates.
Description: New York : PowerKids Press, [2019] | Series: STEM milestones:
    Historic inventions and discoveries | Includes index.
Identifiers: LCCN 2018027013| ISBN 9781538343555 (library bound) | ISBN
    9781538345160 (paperback) | ISBN 9781538345177 (6 pack)
Subjects: LCSH: Darwin, Charles, 1809-1882–Juvenile literature. | Darwin,
    Charles, 1809-1882. On the origin of species–Juvenile literature. |
    Naturalists–England–Biography–Juvenile literature. | Evolution
    (Biology)–Juvenile literature. | Natural selection–Juvenile literature.
Classification: LCC QH31.D2 C5766 2019 | DDC 576.8/2092 [B] –dc23
LC record available at https://lccn.loc.gov/2018027013

CONTENTS

CHANGING OUR UNDERSTANDING

All living things are connected to something in the past. This idea is something that Charles Darwin spent most of his life studying. Darwin was a scientist who was born over 200 years ago. He spent years traveling the world, studying different things in nature and the science behind them. His most famous theory, or explanation for how or why things happen, is known as **evolution** by natural selection.

Darwin used science to prove how living things—both plants and animals—can change over long periods of time and become new kinds of plants and animals. His theory gave **evidence** that helped us further understand where everything comes from. It changed the way that scientists and other people viewed the natural world.

It took Darwin many years to come up with his theory on evolution. It took him even longer to share the idea publicly.

YOUNG AND EDUCATED

Charles Robert Darwin was born on February 12, 1809, in Shrewsbury, England. His father, Robert Darwin, was a successful doctor. His mother, Susannah, died when Charles was eight years old. He had four sisters and one brother. When Darwin was younger, he enjoyed spending time outside, studying plants and collecting beetles.

YOUNG CHARLES DARWIN

Charles Darwin's grandfather, Erasmus Darwin, was a famous scientist, writer, and doctor. He wrote a number of books. One was about botany, which is the study of plants.

ERASMUS DARWIN

In 1817, Charles started going to the Shrewsbury School, a public school in his hometown. In 1825, at only 16, he started attending the University of Edinburgh in Edinburgh, Scotland. He studied to be a doctor there but quickly decided that he didn't want to continue his studies.

GETTING TO KNOW NATURE

Darwin left the University of Edinburgh and began studying at the University of Cambridge in Cambridge, England. He continued to study nature there. One of the subjects he studied at Cambridge was geology. Geology is the study of everything that makes up Earth's **structure**.

In August 1831, Darwin and his geology teacher, Adam Sedgwick, visited Wales to study rock layers. Sedgwick was one of the first modern geologists. Years later, Sedgwick would disagree with Darwin on his ideas of evolution.

Christ's College is a part of the University of Cambridge, which is where Darwin studied. At first, he attended the college to become a **minister**.

ADAM SEDGWICK

CHRIST'S COLLEGE

9

AN IMPORTANT OPPORTUNITY

When Darwin got back from his trip with Sedgwick, he was given the opportunity to travel around the world on a ship called the HMS *Beagle*. He was 22 at the time. His job on the **expedition** was to study nature and geology.

The trip was originally supposed to be two years long. It ended up being five! The ship sailed along the coast of South America, but Darwin was allowed to leave the ship to **explore** the territories farther inland. The ship departed in December 1831 and returned in October 1836. Darwin spent those five years learning things that would lead to his theory of evolution.

FASCINATING FINDINGS

The British government financed the HMS *Beagle* voyage. A British naval officer and scientist named Robert Fitzroy commanded the ship. The purpose of the **voyage** was to travel along the coast of South America to get a better understanding of the area. The *Beagle* made three voyages in the 1800s. Darwin was aboard the second.

Darwin only spent 18 months on the ship. He spent the rest of the five years on land, exploring South America and learning about different plants and animals.

HMS *BEAGLE*

STUDYING THE PAST

Darwin read the works of geologist Charles Lyell while on the ship. Lyell believed that Earth's rocks had been shaped slowly over time. Darwin wondered if living things might also change over time.

GALÁPAGOS GIANT TORTOISE

FASCINATING FINDINGS

Darwin didn't just study finches on the voyage. He collected the bones, skins, and fossils of many different animals he found on the islands and in South America. He found the skull of a large sloth that's **extinct.** He also saw large lizards and tortoises, many of which were only found on the islands. He wrote thousands of pages of notes on his findings!

A GALÁPAGOS FINCH

During his time on the *Beagle* and in South America, Darwin studied fossils he found. Fossils are the remains or traces of living things, usually trapped in rocks. He saw fossils of plants and animals that no longer existed. This showed that species, or kinds of living things, can die out. He studied living animals, too. One place the HMS *Beagle* stopped was the Galápagos Islands off South America. It was here that Darwin began collecting samples of birds called finches.

ADAPTING TO SURVIVE

Darwin studied the finches in more **detail** when he returned to England. Each species had a different beak that was the right shape for the food it ate. He concluded that the finches had **adapted** in ways that made it easier for them to find, catch, and eat the foods that they had available on the islands they lived on.

FASCINATING FINDINGS

There are many things that contribute to Darwin's theory of evolution by natural selection. Over time, an animal's features often change. Some of these changes may help it survive better in the wild. For example, small tree finches eat insects. Their beaks are small and narrow—a good shape for catching their food. The way an animal acts may also be a part of natural selection.

This drawing shows some of the different types of beaks Darwin saw on finches from the Galápagos Islands. Even though these birds are all finches, each has a different type of beak that shows how it adapted to its surroundings.

He noted that animals with useful adaptations could live longer and have more babies with the same **traits**. The animals that didn't have these adaptations would die out over time. The animals that adapted and survived would form new species. He called this idea "natural selection."

TELLING THE WORLD

Darwin married his first cousin, Emma Wedgwood, in 1839. They had 10 children together.

Darwin spent time with his family, but he also spent years working on his theory of evolution by natural selection. He knew it would be **controversial**, so he wanted to make sure he had strong evidence and information to support his ideas. For more than 20 years, he was careful about telling people about his findings. He only told his wife and select scientists who shared his ideas. In time, Darwin decided to write a book explaining his theory. *On the Origin of Species* came out in 1859, when Darwin was 50 years old.

FASCINATING FINDINGS

In *On the Origin of Species,* Darwin talks about the different ways that evolution by natural selection can happen. Sometimes species change in very small ways—for example, the difference in size of the finches' beaks. Sometimes, over many years, species can change in very large ways. These changes may result in the creation of a whole new species.

16

DARWIN IN 1854

Darwin was very sick while he was compiling his notes and writing *On the Origin of Species*. This, along with the death of his daughter, affected how long it took him to publish the book.

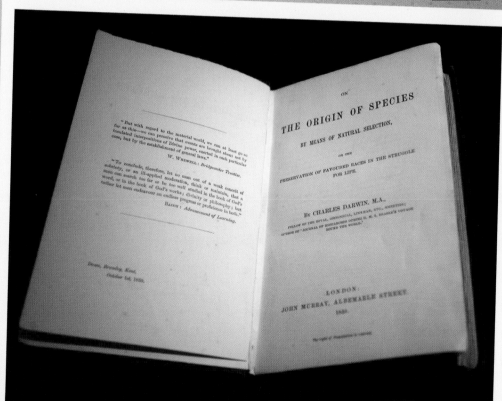

FIRST EDITION OF *ON THE ORIGIN OF SPECIES*

MAKING CONNECTIONS

Darwin released another book, *The Descent of Man*, in 1871. In this book, he argued that people, like all other living things, evolved over time. One of the biggest ideas that he talked about in the book was the idea that humans are closely related to apes, monkeys, and other animals that share similar traits. He thought that certain primates evolved into human beings.

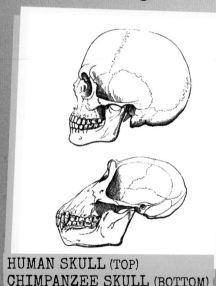

HUMAN SKULL (TOP)
CHIMPANZEE SKULL (BOTTOM)

FASCINATING FINDINGS

The *Descent of Man* gave examples of why Darwin believed that primates were ancestors, or those who came before in the family tree, of humans. He did this by providing information that linked the two by their similarities. Skulls, or bones that form the head and face, in early species of humans were compared to skulls of different animals, showing their similarities.

Some people were upset with Darwin's ideas on evolution. At that time, many people believed that all species were created at the beginning of time and didn't evolve. However, although some people without scientific backgrounds disagreed with his findings, many scientists accepted his theories.

19

A NATURALIST

Charles Darwin was a naturalist. This means that he studied nature and its history. Darwin spent the rest of his life continuing to write and study evolution by natural selection.

Darwin died in 1882 and was buried in London, England. Since his death, scientists have expanded on his findings and continued to draw conclusions on the origins of species and the natural world. Darwin's ideas were very controversial and sometimes unpopular, but his studies have helped us learn more about how species of plants and animals—and the human race itself—came to be.

Darwin wrote a book about emotions in animals and people. He also wrote a book about plants that eat insects.

THE LIFE OF CHARLES DARWIN

February 12, 1809
Charles Robert Darwin is born in Shrewsbury, England.

1817
Darwin starts attending the Shrewsbury School.

1825
Darwin begins attending the University of Edinburgh.

1827
After leaving the University of Edinburgh, Darwin begins studying at Christ's College at the University of Cambridge.

August 1831
Geology professor Adam Sedgwick and Darwin go on a trip to Wales to study rock layers.

December 1831
The HMS *Beagle* departs.

October 1836
The HMS *Beagle* returns.

1839
Darwin marries Emma Wedgwood.

1859
On the Origin of Species is published.

1871
The Descent of Man is published.

1882
Darwin dies and is buried in London, England.

GLOSSARY

adapt: To change to live better in certain surroundings.

controversial: Likely to give rise to disagreement.

detail: A small part or feature.

emotion: A strong feeling.

evidence: Something that shows that something else is true.

evolution: The process of growing and changing over time.

expedition: A trip taken for a certain purpose.

explore: To travel over or through a place to learn more about it.

expression: The act of making thoughts or feelings known.

extinct: No longer existing.

minister: Someone who leads a church and its services.

similarity: Something that makes one person or thing like another.

structure: The way something is built or arranged.

trait: A quality that makes one person or thing different from another.

voyage: A journey.

INDEX

WEBSITES